35 Reasons Healing is God's Will

A manual on participating with God
in the area of Faith, Health, and Healing

Sword Ministries International

Scripture quotations marked (AMP) taken from the Amplified® Bible, Copyright © 1954, 1958, 1962, 1964, 1965, 1987 by The Lockman Foundation. Used by permission. (www.Lockman.org)

Scripture marked (NKJV) taken from the New King James Version®. Copyright © 1982 by Thomas Nelson, Inc. Used by permission. All rights reserved.

35 Reasons Healing is God's Will
Published by:
Sword Ministries International
www.swordministries.org

Copyright ©2016 by Sword Ministries International
All rights reserved.
Reproduction of text in whole or in part without the express written consent by the author is not permitted and is unlawful according to the 1976 United States Copyright Act.

ISBN: 1-889816-52-3

35 Reasons Healing is God's Will

Greetings! In this study we are going to look at 35 areas that show that God's will is to heal and share wisdom on ways we can partake and participate in healing. 2000 years ago Jesus was beaten and whipped; his passion provided the way for each of us to walk in divine health. Let each of the following scriptures bring you into greater revelation of all that Jesus has done for us.

1. God's Medicine - His words

   A. Exodus 15:26 AMP - "saying, "If you will diligently listen *and* pay attention to the voice of the Lord your God, and do what is right in His sight, and listen to His commandments, and keep [foremost in your thoughts and actively obey] all His precepts *and* statutes, then I will not put on you any of the diseases which I have put on the Egyptians; for I am the Lord who heals you."
      I. God is speaking to me now, saying "I am the Lord who heals you." He is watching over his word to perform it.

II. This word contains the ability to produce what it says. He is the Lord who heals me. He is healing me now. This word is full of healing power.
III. I receive this word now. I receive the healing that is in His word now.
IV. Healing is inherent in God's nature.
V. God is in me. My body is the temple of God. My body is the temple of the Lord that heals me. God is bigger than sickness and satan. God is dwelling inside of me now, healing me now.
VI. The Lord who heals me is my shepherd. I do not lack healing.
VII. My body is in contact with the Lord who heals me. My body has to respond to God's healing life and nature at work in me now.
VIII. Healing is in God, and God is in me.
IX. I thank you Father, that Jesus the healer lives in me!

B. Proverbs 4:20-22 AMP - "My son, pay attention to my words *and* be willing to learn; Open your ears to my sayings. Do not let them escape from your sight; Keep them in the center of your heart. For they are life to those who find them, <u>And healing *and* health to all their flesh</u>."
  I. The Hebrew word for "health" in verse 22 is the word "medicine." God's word is medicine to all our flesh. Isaac Leeser's translation of Exodus

15:26 reads: "I the Lord am thy physician." The medicine He prescribes is his word.

Many make the mistake of substituting belief in healing for the actual taking of God's medicine, His Word. They say, "I believe in healing," without actually taking the medicine. What good would it do you to believe in food if you didn't eat it? You would starve. What good would it do you to believe in water if you didn't actually drink any? You would die of thirst. God's word is his medicine.

There are several parallels between God's medicine and natural medicine. First, God's word is a healing agent just as natural medicine is a healing agent or catalyst. In other words, the medicine itself contains the capacity to produce healing. God's word contains inherent within it the capacity - the energy, the ability, and the nature to effect healing in your body.

II. God's Word is health to all my flesh. His Word is medicine to my flesh. "I am the Lord who heals you" is medicine to all my flesh. "I will take sickness away fro the midst of you" is medicine to all my flesh. The Word of God is full of the life of God. That life is saturating my spirit. God's life and healing power is in His Word, and His Word is at work in me now. The Word of God is depositing the life of God and the healing of God into my spirit. That life and health is spreading out of my spirit into every tissue and pore of my body, creating health and soundness. My body has no choice but to respond to the healing in the Word that is being absorbed into me now.

III. We might say that attending to them, inclining your ear to them, and keeping them before your eyes causes them to get in the midst of your heart.

Notice this — it is only as they get in the midst of your heart and stay there that they produce healing in your body. Head knowledge won't do. They are going to have to penetrate to your spirit through mediation - attending, hearing, looking, muttering, musing, pondering - to produce healing in your body. But once they do penetrate, they will surely bring health to all your flesh.

IV. My tongue makes me well. I have what I say.
I say, "The Lord is my Healer."
I say, "He takes sickness away from me."
I say, "No plague can come near my dwelling."
I say, "He heals all my diseases."
What I confess I possess. My words make me well. There is healing power in my words, for they are God's words. I speak health to every muscle, tissue, fiber, and cell in my body. I

release God's healing power with my words into my whole body. Healing is mine.

V. I believe I have received my healing.
Mark 11:24 NKJV says "Therefore I say to you, all things for which you pray and ask, believe that you have received them, and they will be granted you."
You have healed me. I don't consider what I feel. I believed I am healed. You have healed me.
The key to partaking of the life and healing energy in the Word is feeding on it until it penetrates your spirit where it deposits that life and energy.

VI. Secondly, we might say that medicine is no respecter of persons. It will work for anyone who takes it. It is not a matter of God willing or not willing to heal any individual, but whether or not the individual will receive healing by taking the medicine that produces it.

VII. Thirdly, and most importantly, medicine must be taken according to the directions to be effective. Some medicine labels read, 'take internally,' others say 'take externally.' To rub it on your body externally when the directions say to take it internally will not work. To take it after meals when the directions say take it before meals will reduce its effectiveness. To take it once in a while when the directions say three times a day will mean limited results, if any. No matter how good the medicine is, it must be taken according to the directions or it won't work. So it is with God's medicine. It must be taken according to directions for it to work. The directions for taking God's medicine are: No limits! Overdose! Take as much as needed until you are fully healed!

VIII. You can see again that God's way of healing is spiritual. Power is ministered first to your spirit, then distributed to your body. God's medicine must be taking internally.

IX. Instead of wondering whether you have enough faith to be healed, just take the medicine. Feed on God's word several times a day, repeating it over and over again to yourself. The medicine itself will work once you get it inside you.

X. Fourthly, remember that it takes time for medicine to work. Most people give natural medicine a lot of time and patience and money to work. They take the prescription back for refills and more refills. They are diligent about it. They don't just take one dose and expect a miracle. Keep taking God's medicine. Give it time to work.

XI. Take your medicine. Say these scriptures to yourself. Think on what you're saying in your heart. Use them in praise to the Father. His Word is medicine to all your flesh.

C. Psalms 107:20 AMP - "He sent His word and healed them, And rescued them from their destruction."
   I. He sent his word and healed me. His word heals me and delivers me from my destruction. His word frees me from my corruptions.
   II. God's word contains God's ability to perform what it says.
   III. Isaiah 55:10-11 NKJV - "For as the rain comes down, and the snow from heaven, And do not return there, But water the earth, And make it bring forth and bud, That it may give seed to the sower And bread to the eater, So shall My word be that goes forth from My mouth; It shall not return to Me void, But it shall accomplish what I please, And it shall prosper *in the thing* for which I sent it."
   IV. His word is healing me now. His word contains the healing power I need! His word is working in me now. He has sent his word and healed me.

D. Psalms 119:50 AMP - "This is my comfort in my affliction, That Your word has revived me *and* given me life."

E. Proverbs 17:22 AMP - "A happy heart is good medicine *and* a joyful mind causes healing, But a broken spirit dries up the bones."
   I. I have a happy heart. Sickness can't dominate me. Satan can't dominate me. The enemy can't put sickness on me.
   II. I have a merry heart. I'm full of joy. A merry heart works like a medicine. God's medicine is working in me.
   III. The Word itself contains the power to produce what it says, just as when God said, "Let there be light," and there was light. Healing Scriptures contain within them the capacity to produce healing.

Confession: *"Father, I believe that your word is life and healing to my body. I receive your word. Be it unto me according to your word. There is grace for my healing in the word of God. As I meditate on your word, I know that healing is taking place in me now."*

2. **God's Strength** - Strong in the Lord

    A. Proverbs 18:14 AMP - "The spirit of a man <u>sustains him in sickness</u>, But as for a broken spirit, who can bear it?"

    B. Joel 3:10b NKJV - "Let the weak say, '<u>I am strong</u>.'"
        I. Say out loud: "I am strong in the Lord and in the power of his might!"
        II. Say it until you have gotten it!

    C. Nehemiah 8:10 NKJV - "Then he said to them, 'Go your way, eat the fat, drink the sweet, and send portions to those for whom nothing is prepared; for *this* day *is* holy to our Lord. Do not sorrow, for the joy of the Lord is your strength.'"

If we do not spend time in prayer we will not have a lot of joy. Some people do not know that their oil is running low because they have not checked their joy stick. If the devil cannot steal our joy, then he cannot defeat us. The enemy will always try to steal our joy. The devil came to steal, kill, and destroy but Jesus has come that we may have life and have it more abundantly. Jesus came so that we could have joy.

D. Psalms 119:28b NKJV - "Strengthen me according to Your word."

E. Romans 15:13 NKJV - "Now may the God of hope fill you with all joy and peace in believing, that you may <u>abound</u> in hope <u>by the power of the Holy Spirit</u>."

<u>Confession:</u> *"I declare that I am strong in the Lord and in the power of His might. The strength of the Lord is at work in me. God's strength is great especially in the middle of my weakness. I am resting in the Lord's power. I receive strength for the Lord in my body right now."*

3. God's Design: Perfection

A. Psalm 139:14 AMP - "I will give thanks *and* praise to You, for I am fearfully and wonderfully made; Wonderful are Your works, And my soul knows it very well.

B. Genesis 1:26-31 NKJV - "Then God said, "Let Us make man in Our image, according to Our likeness; <u>let them have dominion</u> over the fish of the sea, over the birds of the air, and over the cattle, over all the earth and <u>over every creeping thing that creeps on the earth</u>." So God created man in His *own* image; <u>in the image of God</u> He created him; male and female He created them. Then <u>God blessed them</u>, and God said to them, "Be fruitful and multiply; fill the earth and subdue it; have dominion over the fish of the sea, over the birds of the air, and over every living thing that moves on the earth." And God said, "See, I have given you every herb *that* yields seed which *is* on the face of all the earth, and every tree whose fruit yields seed; to you it shall be for food. Also, to every beast of the earth, to every bird of the air, and to everything that creeps on the earth, in which *there is* life, *I have given* every green herb for food"; and it was so. Then God saw <u>everything</u> that He had made, and indeed *it was* very good. So the evening and the morning were the sixth day."

C. Romans 5:12 AMP - "Therefore, just as sin came into the world through one man, and death through sin, so death spread to all people [no one being able to stop it or escape its power], because they all sinned."

Confession: *"I acknowledge that God is my creator and I know that God does not make junk. My design is very good. I was created in the very image of God. I bear his image and in the name of Jesus that good image is fully restored in me. Disease and disorder cannot continue in my body. My body was designed with good functionality and wonderful working parts. I am destined for a glorified body and not a broken down vessel."*

4. Origin of Sickness and Disease

A. Romans 5:12 AMP - "Therefore, just as sin came into the world through one man, and death through sin, so death spread to all people [no one being able to stop it or escape its power], because they all sinned."
   I. Sickness is the result of sin and its presence in the world is directly traced to the influence of satan.

B. Romans 6:23 NKJV - "For the wages of sin *is* death, but the gift of God *is* eternal life in Christ Jesus our Lord."
   I. Death is sin that has matured, if there had been no sin in the world there would have been no sickness or death.

Confession: *"Death came into this world through sin, therefore I declare that in Christ my sins have been forgiven and that the grace of the Lord Jesus Christ has canceled my appointment with death. His stripes have brought about my healing. The gift of God is eternal life in Christ Jesus and that life is at work in me now. My inheritance comes from the Lord and in him there is no sickness and no disease. I therefore reject any work of sin in my life and reject its effects of sickness and disease in my body."*

5. Sickness is the Work of the Devil

A. Job 2:7 NKJV - "So Satan went out from the presence of the Lord, and struck Job with painful boils from the sole of his foot to the crown of his head."

B. John 10:10 AMP - " The thief comes only in order to steal and kill and destroy. I came that they may have *and* enjoy life, and have it in abundance [to the full, till it overflows]."
   I. 1 John 3:8 NKJV - "He who sins is of the devil, for the devil has sinned from the beginning. For this purpose the Son of God was manifested, that He might destroy the works of the devil."
   II. AMPC - "The reason the Son of God was made manifest (visible) was to undo (destroy, loosen, and dissolve) the works the devil [has done].
   III. Young - "that he may break up the works of the devil;"
   IV. Basic English - "and the Son of God was seen on earth so that he might put an end to the works of the Evil One."
   V. Wand - "That he might neutralize what the Devil has done."
   VI. Wuest - "That he might bring to naught the works of the devil."

VII. Jordan - "That he might break up the Devil's doings."
VIII. Jerusalem - "To lead a sinful life is to belong to the devil, since the devil was a sinner from the beginning. It was to undo all that the devil has done that the Son of God appeared."
IX. Phillips - "Now the Son of God came to the earth with the express purpose of liquidating the devil's activities."
X. Concordant - "That He should be annulling the acts of the Adversary."

Sickness is a work of the devil. Jesus came to destroy the works of the devil. Sickness has been dissolved, broken up, annulled, undone, liquidated as far as I am concerned. Jesus put sickness to an end for me. The activities of the devil have been liquidated.

C. Luke 9:56 NKJV - "For the Son of Man did not come to destroy men's lives but to save *them*."

D. Luke 13:16 AMP - "And this woman, a daughter (descendant) of Abraham whom Satan has bound for eighteen long years, should she not have been released from this bond on the Sabbath day?"
   I. Satan can't bind me with sickness. I have been delivered from Satan's dominion and translated

into the kingdom of the Son of God (Colossians 1:13). Sickness is ungodly. Sickness is of the devil. The devil is a defeated foe who Jesus stripped of authority over me (Colossians 2:15, Hebrews 2:14).

II. Satan can't do this to me. I resist him in Jesus' name.
I am delivered.
I am free.
I have been loosed.
I am no longer fettered.
I am now rid of my infirmity.
My bondage is at an end!
It is right for me to be completely free, for I am a child of Abraham and Abraham's blessings are mine (Galatians 3:14-29).

III. Healing is part of the covenant. I am under the covenant. Healing is mine. Healing belongs to me. It is my rightful possession. I have a right to be released.

IV. Satan, I demand my rights now! Take your hands off my body!

E. Acts 10:38 AMP - "how God anointed Jesus of Nazareth with the Holy Spirit and with great power; and He went around doing good and healing all who were oppressed by the devil, because God was with Him."

I. Sickness is oppression of the devil. Satan can't oppress me with sickness because I have been delivered from his authority (Colossians 1:13).
II. I have authority to tread on satan and demons and all the power the enemy possesses. I tread on sickness!
Satan can't lord over me with foul disease. Sickness cannot do this to me. It has visited the wrong one. Healing is mine!
III. The same power that raised Jesus from the dead is at work in me. It is healing power because He is the Lord who heals me. Healing power is at work in me and I am free.
IV. 1 Peter 5:8-9 NKJV - "Be sober, be vigilant; because[a] your adversary the devil walks about like a roaring lion, seeking whom he may devour. Resist him, steadfast in the faith, knowing that the same sufferings are experienced by your brotherhood in the world."
V. I stand immovable against sickness in Jesus' name. I refuse to accept it.
VI. Ephesians 4:27 AMPC - "Leave no [such] room *or* foothold for the devil [give no opportunity to him]."
VII. Since sickness and disease are of the devil I refuse to give place to them! Satan, you can not put that on my body. I say "no," and I mean "no!"

    VIII. No sickness or disease comes near my dwelling place. You have the wrong address.
    IX. You have no place in me or my body. I belong to God, therefore sickness has no choice but to leave now!

F. Isaiah 54:16-17 AMP "Behold, I have created the smith who blows on the fire of coals and who produces a weapon for its purpose; and I have created the devastator to destroy. But no weapon that is formed against you shall prosper, and every tongue that shall rise against you in judgment you shall show to be in the wrong. This [peace, righteousness, security, triumph over opposition] is the heritage of the servants of the Lord [those in whom the ideal Servant of the Lord is reproduced]; this is the righteousness *or* the vindication which they obtain from Me [this is that which I impart to them as their justification], says the Lord."

G. Remember that the devil's food is the "dust of the earth" but we are "seated with Christ, far above all powers and principalities."

Confession: *"The Son of God was manifested to destroy every work of the Devil. In Christ I have been translated out of the kingdom of darkness and into the kingdom of God's marvelous light. Every work of the devil manifesting in sickness and disease in my life is illegitimate and must end now. The Love of God has lifted me above the onslaught of the enemy and seated me with Christ above the power of the evil spirits. In Christ I am free from every work of the enemy. Sickness and disease have no choice but to leave me now."*

6. Covenant of Healing

A. Exodus 15:26 NKJV - "and said, "If you diligently heed the voice of the Lord your God and do what is right in His sight, give ear to His commandments and keep all His statutes, I will put none of the diseases on you which I have brought on the Egyptians. For I *am* the Lord who heals you."

B. Deuteronomy 7:12b AMPC - "the Lord your God will keep with you the covenant and the steadfast love which He swore to your fathers."

C. Deuteronomy 7:15a AMPC - "And the Lord will take away from you all sickness, and none of the evil diseases of Egypt which you knew will He put upon you,"
  I. The Lord is taking away from me all sickness.
  II. His Word contains the ability to do what it says, His word will not return vow but will accomplish what it was sent to do.
  III. The Lord is taking away from me every trace of weakness and deficiency.

D. Exodus 23:25 AMP - "You shall serve the Lord your God; He shall bless your bread and water, and I will take sickness from your midst."

I. 3 John 2 AMPC - "Beloved, I pray that you may prosper in every way and [that your body] may keep well, even as [I know] your soul keeps well *and* prospers."
   II. I am prospering and I am in health even as my soul prospers because it is God's will for me. God is at work in me to do his will and pleasure (Philippians 2:13).
   III. Jehovah-Rapha is at work in me, healing me.
   IV. God is at work healing me. God is greater than the devil. Healing is greater than sickness.

   E. Say this: "I am in covenant relationship with an immortal, resurrected man. As He is, so am I in this world."

Confession: *"I am a partaker of the Divine Nature through the New Covenant that was ratified in Christ's blood. The Lord is taking away from me all sickness and all weakness. God is at work in me to do his will. The will of God to prosper me and give me a good future is the greatest power at work in my life. I receive now the healing/salvation benefits of being in Covenant with the Lord Jesus Christ."*

7. Unchanging Redemptive Names of God

A. Jehovah Rapha - The Lord our Healer
  I. Matthew 9:12 AMP - "But when Jesus heard it, He replied, Those who are strong *and* well (healthy) have no need of a physician, but those who are weak *and* sick."
  II. Exodus 15:26 NKJV - "Saying, If you will diligently hearken to the voice of the Lord your God and will do what is right in His sight, and will listen to *and* obey His commandments and keep all His statutes, I will put none of the diseases upon you which I brought upon the Egyptians, for I am the Lord Who heals you."
  III. The Lord is our physician. The ministry of Jesus is exactly to those who are weak and sick.

B. Jehovah Ra-ah - The Lord is our Shepherd
  I. John 10:4 NKJV - "And when he brings out his own sheep, he goes before them; and the sheep follow him, for they know his voice."
  II. Psalm 23:1-3 AMP - "The Lord is my Shepherd [to feed, guide, and shield me], I shall not lack. He makes me lie down in [fresh, tender] green pastures; He leads me beside the still *and* restful waters. He refreshes *and* restores my life (my self); He leads me in the paths of righteousness

[uprightness and right standing with Him—not for my earning it, but] for His name's sake."
III. Jesus goes before us and leads us into a healthy place.

C. Jehovah Jireh - The Lord our Provider
I. Genesis 22:14 NKJV - "And Abraham called the name of the place, The-Lord-Will-Provide; as it is said *to* this day, "In the Mount of the Lord it shall be provided."
II. Philippians 4:19 AMP - "And my God will liberally supply (fill to the full) your every need according to His riches in glory in Christ Jesus."
III. Just as God provided the bronze serpent on the pole in the dessert for the children of Israel to be healed so we look to Jesus now for our healing.

D. Jehovah Nissi - The Lord our Banner (Victory)
I. Exodus 17:15 NKJV - "And Moses built an altar and called its name, The-Lord-Is-My-Banner;"
II. 1 Corinthians 15:57 AMP - "But thanks be to God, Who gives us the victory [making us conquerors] through our Lord Jesus Christ."
III. 2 Corinthians 2:14 AMP - "But thanks be to God, Who in Christ always leads us in triumph [as trophies of Christ's victory] and through us

spreads *and* makes evident the fragrance of the knowledge of God everywhere,"
    IV. In Christ we obtain victory over every enemy which includes the work of sickness and disease.

E. Jehovah Tsidkenu - The Lord our Righteousness
    I. Jeremiah 33:16 AMP - "In those days Judah shall be saved and Jerusalem shall dwell safely. And this is the name by which it will be called, The Lord is Our Righteousness (our Rightness, our Justice)."
    II. 2 Corinthians 5:21 NKJV - "For He made Him who knew no sin *to be* sin for us, that we might become the righteousness of God in Him."

F. Jehovah Shalom - The Lord our Peace
    I. Judges 6:24 NKJV - "So Gideon built an altar there to the Lord, and called it The-Lord-*Is*-Peace. To this day it *is* still in Ophrah of the Abiezrites."
    II. John 14:27 AMP - "Peace I leave with you; My [own] peace I now give *and* bequeath to you. Not as the world gives do I give to you. Do not let your hearts be troubled, neither let them be afraid. [Stop allowing yourselves to be agitated and disturbed; and do not permit yourselves to

be fearful and intimidated and cowardly and unsettled.]"
   III. Philippians 4:7 NKJV - " and the peace of God, which surpasses all understanding, will guard your hearts and minds through Christ Jesus."

G. Jehovah Shammah - The Lord who is Present
   I. Ezekiel 48:35 NKJV - "All the way around *shall be* eighteen thousand *cubits;* and the name of the city from *that* day *shall be:* THE LORD *IS* THERE."
   II. Hebrews 13:5 NKJV - "*Let your* conduct *be* without covetousness; *be* content with such things as you have. For He Himself has said, "I will never leave you nor forsake you."
   III. In the Amplified Translation Hebrews 13:5 says: "I will not, I will not, I will not in any degree leave you helpless *nor* forsake *nor* let you down (relax My hold on you)! [Assuredly not!]"

Confession: *"I thank you Father that the Lord Jesus Christ identified himself as a physician sent for the weak and the sick. You have always been revealing Yourself as a Healer and Helper. The Lord is my physician and I receive his work in my life now to heal and strengthen me."*

8. Sickness is Part of the Curse

A. Galatians 3:13 NKJV - "Christ has redeemed us from the curse of the law, having become a curse for us (for it is written, "Cursed *is* everyone who hangs on a tree")."
   I. Christ has redeemed me from the curse of the law.
   II. The curse of the law is found in Deuteronomy 28. The curse for breaking God's law includes sickness.
   III. Sickness and disease are part of the curse of the law therefore Christ has redeemed me from sickness and disease. I am liberated, I am ransomed, I am free from disease.
   IV. Confess specific disease: "I am redeemed from _____."
   V. Christ has redeemed me- bought me back, brought me back, and set me free from all sickness and disease.

B. Proverbs 26:2 NKJV - "Like a flitting sparrow, like a flying swallow, So a curse without cause shall not alight."

Confession: *"The curse of the law brings sickness but Christ has redeemed me from the curse of the law. Sickness has no authority in my life and I reject all of its advances and manifestations. Christ has set me free."*

9. Healing In the Types of Redemption

A. Passover Lamb
  I. 1 Corinthians 5:7 AMP - "Purge (clean out) the old leaven that you may be fresh (new) dough, still uncontaminated [as you are], for Christ, our Passover [Lamb], has been sacrificed."

B. Cleansing Ceremony of the Leper
  I. Leviticus 14:1-2 NKJV - "Then the Lord spoke to Moses, saying, "This shall be the law of the leper for the day of his cleansing: He shall be brought to the priest."

C. Year of Jubilee
  I. Leviticus 25:8 NKJV - " 'And you shall count seven sabbaths of years for yourself, seven times seven years; and the time of the seven sabbaths of years shall be to you forty-nine years."
  II. Luke 4:18-19 AMP - "The Spirit of the Lord [is] upon Me, because He has anointed Me [the Anointed One, the Messiah] to preach the good news (the Gospel) to the poor; He has sent Me to announce release to the captives and recovery of sight to the blind, to send forth as delivered those who are oppressed [who are downtrodden, bruised, crushed, and broken down by

calamity], To proclaim the accepted *and* acceptable year of the Lord [the day [a]when salvation and the free favors of God profusely abound].

D. Atonement for the Plague
   I. Numbers 16:47-48 NKJV - "Then Aaron took *it* as Moses commanded, and ran into the midst of the assembly; and already the plague had begun among the people. So he put in the incense and made atonement for the people. And he stood between the dead and the living; so the plague was stopped."

E. Serpent on the Pole
   I. Numbers 21:4-9 AMP - "And they journeyed from Mount Hor by the way to the Red Sea, to go around the land of Edom, and the people became impatient (depressed, much discouraged), because [of the trials] of the way. And the people spoke against God and against Moses, Why have you brought us out of Egypt to die in the wilderness? For there is no bread, neither is there any water, and we loathe this light (contemptible, unsubstantial) manna. Then the Lord sent fiery (burning) serpents among the people; and they bit the people, and many Israelites died. And the people came to Moses,

and said, We have sinned, for we have spoken against the Lord and against you; pray to the Lord, that He may take away the serpents from us. So Moses prayed for the people. And the Lord said to Moses, Make a fiery serpent [of bronze] and set it on a pole; and everyone who is bitten, when he looks at it, shall live. And Moses made a serpent of bronze and put it on a pole, and if a serpent had bitten any man, when he looked to the serpent of bronze [attentively, expectantly, with a steady and absorbing gaze], he lived."

II. John 3:14 AMP - "And just as Moses lifted up the serpent in the desert [on a pole], so must [so it is necessary that] the Son of Man be lifted up [on the cross],"

III. He took all your sickness and disease on the cross!

IV. Isaiah 53:4-5 NKJV - "Surely He has borne our griefs And carried our sorrows; Yet we esteemed Him stricken, Smitten by God, and afflicted. But He *was* wounded for our transgressions, *He was* bruised for our iniquities; The chastisement for our peace *was* upon Him, And by His stripes we are healed."

Confession: *"The scriptures are full of references to the fact that Jesus Christ is my healer. I receive the testimony of scripture and the testimony of the Holy Spirit that I am healed by the stripes that Jesus bore. I am healed and every ailment must submit to the Lordship of Jesus Christ in my life right now."*

10. God's Will in Heaven

A. Isaiah 33:24a AMPC - "And no inhabitant [of Zion] will say, I am sick;"

B. Matthew 6:9-10 NKJV - "In this manner, therefore, pray: Our Father in heaven, Hallowed be Your name. Your kingdom come. Your will be done On earth as *it is* in heaven."

C. Revelation 21:4 AMP - "God will wipe away every tear from their eyes; and death shall be no more, neither shall there be anguish (sorrow and mourning) nor grief nor pain any more, for the old conditions *and* the former order of things have passed away."

D. Deuteronomy 11:21 NKJV - "that your days and the days of your children may be multiplied in the land of which the Lord swore to your fathers to give them, like the days of the heavens above the earth."

E. There is no sickness or disease in Heaven!

Confession: *"The Lord teaches His disciples to pray that God's will would be done on the earth just as it is carried out in Heaven. Therefore I declare that just as there is no sickness, disease, or death in Heaven so sickness, disease, and death have no rightful claim in my life here and now. I resist every work in my life that does not find it's origin and mirror in the reality of Heaven."*

11. First Fruits of our Inheritance

A. Philippians 3:20 NKJV - "For our citizenship is in heaven, from which we also eagerly wait for the Savior, the Lord Jesus Christ,"

B. Romans 8:23 NKJV - "Not only *that,* but we also who have the first-fruits of the Spirit, even we ourselves groan within ourselves, eagerly waiting for the adoption, the redemption of our body."

C. Ephesians 1:13 AMP - "In Him you also who have heard the Word of Truth, the glad tidings (Gospel) of your salvation, and have believed in *and* adhered to *and* relied on Him, were stamped with the seal of the long-promised Holy Spirit."

D. Hebrews 11:39-40 AMP - "And all of these, though they won divine approval by [means of] their faith, did not receive the fulfillment of what was promised, Because God had us in mind *and* had something better *and* greater in view for us, so that they [these heroes and heroines of faith] should not come to perfection apart from us [before we could join them]."

Confession: *"I declare that healing is mine through the Spirit of Adoption. The Holy Spirit in me is the guarantee of my salvation. The Lord's salvation is not just from sin but from sin's ultimate destination: death. The salvation of the Lord is at work in me now healing and redeeming every aspect of my being."*

12. The Good Shepherd

A. Exodus 34:4-11 AMP - "So Moses cut two tables of stone like the first, and he rose up early in the morning and went up on Mount Sinai, as the Lord had commanded him, and took in his hand two tables of stone. And the Lord descended in the cloud and stood with him there and proclaimed the name of the Lord. And the Lord passed by before him, and proclaimed, The Lord! the Lord! a God merciful and gracious, slow to anger, and abundant in loving-kindness and truth, Keeping mercy *and* loving-kindness for thousands, forgiving iniquity and transgression and sin, but Who will by no means clear the guilty, visiting the iniquity of the fathers upon the children and the children's children, to the third and fourth generation. And Moses made haste to bow his head toward the earth and worshiped. And he said, If now I have found favor *and* loving-kindness in Your sight, O Lord, let the Lord, I pray You, go in the midst of us, although it is a stiff-necked people, and pardon our iniquity and our sin, and take us for Your inheritance. And the Lord said, Behold, I lay down [afresh the terms of the mutual agreement between Israel and Me] a covenant. Before all your people I will do marvels (wonders, miracles) such as have not been wrought *or* created in all the earth or in any nation; and all the people among whom you are shall see the work of the Lord; for it is a terrible thing [fearful and full of awe] that I will do with you. Observe what I command you this day. Behold, I drive out before you the Amorite, Canaanite, Hittite, Perizzite, Hivite, and Jebusite."

B. Matthew 12:11-12 NKJV - "Then He said to them, "What man is there among you who has one sheep, and if it falls into a pit on the Sabbath, will not lay hold of it and lift *it* out? Of how much more value then is a man than a sheep? Therefore it is lawful to do good on the Sabbath."

C. Psalms 23:1-6 AMP - "The Lord is my Shepherd [to feed, to guide and to shield me], I shall not want. He lets me lie down in green pastures; He leads me beside the still *and* quiet waters. He refreshes *and* restores my soul (life); He leads me in the paths of righteousness for His name's sake. Even though I walk through the [sunless] valley of the shadow of death, I fear no evil, for You are with me; Your rod [to protect] and Your staff [to guide], they comfort *and* console me. You prepare a table before me in the presence of my enemies. You have anointed *and* refreshed my head with oil; My cup overflows. Surely goodness and mercy *and* unfailing love shall follow me all the days of my life, And I shall dwell

forever [throughout all my days] in the house *and* in the presence of the Lord."
I. The Lord who Heals me is my Shepherd. I do not lack healing.

Confession: *"The Lord is my shepherd and I do not lack for healing. The Lord who heals me is looking out for me. I do not fear evil because the great physician is my attending shepherd. Goodness, mercy, and unfailing love follow me every where I go. I live constantly in the presence of the Lord."*

13. The Children's Bread

A. 1 Timothy 5:8 AMP - "If anyone fails to provide for his own, and especially for those of his own family, he has denied the faith [by disregarding its precepts] and is worse than an unbeliever [who fulfills his obligation in these matters]."

B. Luke 11:3 NKJV - "Give us day by day our daily bread."

C. Matthew 15:26-27 AMP - "And He replied, "It is not good (appropriate, fair) to take the children's bread and throw it to the pet dogs." She said, "Yes, Lord; but even the pet dogs eat the crumbs that fall from their [young] masters' table."

Confession: *"Healing is the children's bread. As a child of God, Healing is my daily portion. I receive healing for this day right now. My Heavenly Father always provides for his own family and I am not lacking provision for healing. I receive what my Father has provided for me right now."*

14. The Fatherhood of God

A. Psalms 103:2-3 NKJV - "Bless the Lord, O my soul, And forget not all His benefits: Who forgives all your iniquities, Who heals all your diseases,"
   I. Bless the Lord, Jehovah-Rapha, O my soul!
   II. I praise you Father, you forgive all my sin, all my faults, all my failures and disobedience. You heal all my diseases!
   III. Healing belongs to me as part of the New Covenant. Healing is my redemptive right.
   IV. A benefit is a condition of a contract, not a bonus thrown in as something extra at the discretion of the employer.

B. Matthew 7:9-11 AMP - " Or what man is there among you who, if his son asks for bread, will [instead] give him a stone? Or if he asks for a fish, will [instead] give him a snake? If you then, evil (sinful by nature) as you are, know how to give good *and* advantageous gifts to your children, how much more will your Father who is in heaven [perfect as He is] give what is good *and* advantageous to those who keep on asking Him."

C. Romans 8:15 AMP - "For you have not received a spirit of slavery leading again to fear [of God's judgment], but you have received the Spirit of adoption as sons [the Spirit producing sonship] by which we [joyfully] cry, "Abba! Father!"

Confession: *"The Holy Spirit in me testifies that I am a child of God. God is a good Father and always gives what is good and advantageous to those who ask of Him. Today I receive what my Heavenly Father has provided for me. God's provision is to my advantage and I receive it now. Sickness and disease bow to the reality of God's fatherhood in my life. I am a child of the Lord who Heals."*

15. The Plan of Redemption

A. Isaiah 53:4-5 NKJV - "Surely He has borne our griefs And carried our sorrows; Yet we esteemed Him stricken, Smitten by God, and afflicted. But He *was* wounded for our transgressions, *He was* bruised for our iniquities; The chastisement for our peace *was* upon Him, And by His stripes we are healed.
   I. He bore my sickness and disease and carried my pain. He bore them and carried them away to a distance.
   II. I don't have to bear what he bore for me. I refuse to bear what he bore for me.
   III. Satan cannot put on me what Jesus bore for me. By his stripes I am healed.
   IV. My diseases went to the cross with Jesus and died with him there.

B. 1 Peter 2:24 AMP - "He personally carried our sins in His body on the cross [willingly offering Himself on it, as on an altar of sacrifice], so that we might die to sin [becoming immune from the penalty and power of sin] and live for righteousness; for by His wounds you [who believe] have been healed."
   I. By his stripes I have been healed. Healing belongs to me. I was healed 2000 years ago by the stripes Jesus bore.

    II. I'm not trying to get healing, i've already got healing because by his stripes I have been healed.

  C. Matthew 8:17 NKJV - "When evening had come, they brought to Him many who were demon-possessed. And He cast out the spirits with a word, and healed all who were sick, that it might be fulfilled which was spoken by Isaiah the prophet, saying: "He Himself took our infirmities And bore our sicknesses.

Confession: *"In accordance with the Plan of Redemption I reject every work of sin, sickness, and disease that would come against my body. I refuse to bear what Jesus has already bore for me. My sin and sickness was nailed to the cross with Jesus and it died there. Jesus rose from the dead but my sickness remains dead. I am healed through the wounds that Jesus suffered at the cross."*

16. Because of the Love and Compassion of the Lord

A. Matthew 15:32 NKJV - " Now Jesus called His disciples to *Himself* and said, "I have compassion on the multitude, because they have now continued with Me three days and have nothing to eat. And I do not want to send them away hungry, lest they faint on the way."

B. Matthew 20:34 AMP - "Moved with compassion, Jesus touched their eyes; and immediately they regained their sight and followed Him [as His disciples].

C. Luke 15:20 NKJV - "And he arose and came to his father. But when he was still a great way off, his father saw him and had compassion, and ran and fell on his neck and kissed him."

D. James 5:11b NKJV - "that the Lord is very compassionate and merciful."

Confession: *"I declare that the Lord is full of compassion and mercy for me. The Lord sees my ailments and is moved by compassion. I receive the miraculous that always accompanies Godly compassion in my body this day."*

17. The Ministry of Jesus

A. Matthew 21:14 NKJV - "Then *the* blind and *the* lame came to Him in the temple, and He healed them."

B. John 6:38 NKJV - "For I have come down from heaven, not to do My own will, but the will of Him who sent Me.

C. Matthew 8:2-3 AMPC - "And behold, a leper came up to Him and, prostrating himself, worshiped Him, saying, Lord, if You are willing, You are able to cleanse me by curing me. And He reached out His hand and touched him, saying, I am willing; be cleansed by being cured. And instantly his leprosy was cured *and* cleansed."
   I. God wants me cured and cleansed.
   II. Healing is the will of God.
   III. God is at work in me right now to will and to do his good pleasure (Philippians 2:13).

D. Matthew 8:16 NKJV - "When evening had come, they brought to Him many who were demon-possessed. And He cast out the spirits with a word, and healed all who were sick, that it might be fulfilled which was spoken by Isaiah the prophet, saying: "He Himself took our infirmities And bore our sicknesses."

    I. He himself took my infirmity and bore my sickness. He took them and removed them.
    II. Disease is not mine. Healing is mine.
    III. I refuse to bear what Jesus already bore for me.
    IV. I will not tolerate sickness.
    V. Jesus removed them and I refuse to have them any longer.

E. Mark 5:25-34 NKJV - "Now a certain woman had a flow of blood for twelve years, and had suffered many things from many physicians. She had spent all that she had and was no better, but rather grew worse. When she heard about Jesus, she came behind *Him* in the crowd and touched His garment. For she said, "If only I may touch His clothes, I shall be made well." Immediately the fountain of her blood was dried up, and she felt in *her* body that she was healed of the affliction. And Jesus, immediately knowing in Himself that power had gone out of Him, turned around in the crowd and said, "Who touched My clothes?" But His disciples said to Him, "You see the multitude thronging You, and You say, 'Who touched Me?'" And He looked around to see her who had done this thing. But the woman, fearing and trembling, knowing what had happened to her, came and fell down before Him and told Him the whole truth. And He said to her, "Daughter, your faith has made you well. Go in peace, and be healed of your affliction."

    I. Her faith made her whole and my faith makes me whole. I have faith because I am a believer.

    II. I believe I receive my healing and my faith makes me whole.

    III. The power that raised Christ from the dead is at work in me (Ephesians 1:19).

    IV. My faith puts that power into active operation in my body. Disease has no chance for survival in my body.

    V. The power that raised Jesus from the dead is at work in me and it is irresistible. That power is greater than sickness and disease. That power is flowing in me and makes me whole.

F. Acts 10:36-38 AMP - "You know the message which He sent to the sons of Israel, announcing the good news of peace through Jesus Christ, who is Lord of all— you know the things that have taken place throughout Judea, starting in Galilee after the baptism preached by John— how God anointed Jesus of Nazareth with the Holy Spirit and with great power; and He went around doing good and healing all who were oppressed by the devil, because God was with Him.

G. Acts 5:12 AMP - "At the hands of the apostles many signs and wonders (attesting miracles) were *continually* taking place among the people. And by common consent they all met together [at the temple] in [the covered porch called] Solomon's portico."

Confession: *"The Ministry of Jesus was one of regularly healing the sick. Jesus came to do the will of God the Father who sent him. Based on the ministry of Jesus I believe that it is God's will to heal all who are sick and oppressed. I receive the ministry of Jesus in my own body this day by the grace of the Holy Spirit."*

18. Authority over Sickness and Disease in the Name of Jesus

A. Matthew 10:1 AMP - "Jesus summoned His twelve disciples and gave them authority *and* power over unclean spirits, to cast them out, and to heal every kind of disease and every kind of sickness.

B. Mark 16:17-18 AMP - "And these attesting signs will accompany those who believe: in My name they will drive out demons; they will speak in new languages; they will pick up serpents, and if they drink anything deadly, it will not hurt them; they will lay hands on the sick, and they will get well."
   I. The name of Jesus is greater than sickness.
   II. Say: "In the name of Him who conquered sin, sickness, and satan, I command disease to leave my body now. Satan, I cast you out in Jesus' name. You can't do this to me. I am free."

C. Matthew 28:18 NKJV - "And Jesus came and spoke to them, saying, "All authority has been given to Me in heaven and on earth."

D. Luke 9:1 NKJV - "Then He called His twelve disciples together and gave them power and authority over all demons, and to cure diseases."

E. Luke 4:18 NKJV - "The Spirit of the Lord *is* upon Me, Because He has anointed Me, To preach the gospel to *the* poor; He has sent Me to heal the brokenhearted, To proclaim liberty to *the* captives And recovery of sight to *the* blind, *To* set at liberty those who are oppressed;"

F. Luke 10:19 AMPC - "Behold! I have given you authority *and* power to trample upon serpents and scorpions, and [physical and mental strength and ability] over all the power that the enemy [possesses]; and nothing shall in any way harm you."

  I. Sickness is a power of the devil (Acts 10:38). I trample on all the power of the devil.
  II. I tread every evil underfoot. I stomp on disease. I trample sickness.
  III. The Lord Jesus Christ himself has given me authority over all the power of the enemy.
  IV. I have authority over the power of sickness.
  V. Say: " Sickness, you have no right to dominate me. Get out of my body in Jesus' name."
  VI. Sickness and disease are under my feet because I am seated with Christ above all the power of the enemy (Ephesians 2:6).

G. John 14:12-14 AMPC - "I assure you, most solemnly I tell you, if anyone steadfastly believes in Me, he will himself be able to do the things that I

do; and he will do even greater things than these, because I go to the Father. And I will do [I Myself will grant] whatever you ask in My Name [as presenting all that I Am], so that the Father may be glorified *and* extolled in (through) the Son. [Yes] I will grant [I Myself will do for you] whatever you shall ask in My Name [as presenting all that I Am]."
- I. The name of Jesus takes the place of Jesus. Jesus is the resurrected healing Lord.
- II. Say: " In the name of Jesus I command disease to leave my body. My body is healed in Jesus' name."
- III. His name, through faith in his name, gives me perfect soundness (Acts 3:16).

H. Ephesians 1:21-22 AMP - "far above all rule and authority and power and dominion [whether angelic or human], and [far above] every name that is named [above every title that can be conferred], not only in this age *and* world but also in the one to come. And He put all things [in every realm] in subjection under Christ's feet, and appointed Him as [supreme and authoritative] head over all things in the church,"

Confession: *"The Lord Jesus Christ has given me authority over the enemy and authority over every kind of sickness and every kind of disease. I accept and operate in my God given authority and resist every work of the enemy in my life. In Christ I am completely authorized to eradicate every work of satan."*

19. Prayers of Healing

A. Numbers 12:13 NKJV - "So Moses cried out to the Lord, saying, "Please heal her, O God, I pray!"

B. Psalms 6:2 AMP - "Have mercy on me *and* be gracious to me, O Lord, for I am weak (faint, frail); Heal me, O Lord, for my bones are dismayed *and* anguished."

C. James 5:14-15 AMP - "Is anyone among you sick? He must call for the elders (spiritual leaders) of the church and they are to pray over him, anointing him with oil in the name of the Lord; and the prayer of faith will restore the one who is sick, and the Lord will raise him up; and if he has committed sins, he will be forgiven."
   I. The prayer of faith has made me whole.
   II. The Lord is raising me up, I cannot stay down.
   III. I believe I received when I prayed, and my faith makes me whole.

D. Psalms 38:3-22 AMP - "There is no soundness in my flesh because of Your indignation; There is no health in my bones because of my sin. For my iniquities have gone over my head [like the waves of a flood]; As a heavy burden they weigh too much for me. My wounds are loathsome and foul Because of my foolishness. I am bent over and greatly bowed down; I go about mourning all day long. For my sides are filled with burning, And there is no health in my flesh. I am numb and greatly bruised [deadly cold and completely worn out]; I groan because of the disquiet *and* moaning of my heart. Lord, all my desire is before You; And my sighing is not hidden from You. My heart throbs violently, my strength fails me; And as for the light of my eyes, even that has also gone from me. My loved ones and my friends stand aloof from my plague; And my neighbors stand far away. Those who seek my life lay snares *for me*, And those who seek to injure me threaten mischievous things *and* destruction; They devise treachery all the day long. But I, like a deaf man, do not hear; I am like a mute man who does not open his mouth. Yes, I am like a man who does not hear, In whose mouth are no arguments. For in You, O Lord, I hope; You will answer, O Lord my God. For I pray, "May they not rejoice over me, Who, when my foot slips, would boast against me." For I am ready to fall; My sorrow is continually before me. For I do confess my guilt *and* iniquity; I am filled with anxiety because of my sin. But my [numerous] enemies are vigorous and strong, And those who hate me without cause are many. They repay evil for good, they attack *and* try to kill me, Because I follow what is good. Do not abandon me, O Lord; O my God, do not be far from me. Make haste to help me, O Lord, my Salvation.

Confession: *"I know that the Lord hears my prayers and all of my petitions. When I pray it is not in vain. I expect my prayers to be heard and answered. Thank you Heavenly Father that you hear my words and answer me before I can even get them all out. I will not be guilty of 'not having' due to 'not asking.' Healing is the will of God so I ask without hesitation for healing. When I pray for healing, it springs forth quickly."*

20. Ordinance of Laying on Hands

A. Hebrews 6:2 NKJV - "of the doctrine of baptisms, of laying on of hands, of resurrection of the dead, and of eternal judgment."

B. James 5:14 AMP - "Is anyone among you sick? He must call for the elders (spiritual leaders) of the church and they are to pray over him, anointing him with oil in the name of the Lord;"

C. Matthew 8:2-3 AMP - "And a leper came up to Him and bowed down before Him, saying, "Lord, if You are willing, You are able to make me clean (well)." Jesus reached out His hand and touched him, saying, "I am willing; be cleansed." Immediately his leprosy was cleansed."

D. Mark 16:18b NKJV - "they will lay hands on the sick, and they will recover."
   I. Say: "The Bible says you shall lay hands on the sick and they will recover. So in obedience to the word, I lay my hands on you in the name of Jesus Christ our Lord."

Confession: *"The same Spirit that raised Christ from the dead lives in me. When I lay my hands on the sick, they recover. Greater is He that is in me than any sickness, disease, or devil that is in the world. The power of God in me is contagious and overtakes everything that it comes into contact with. Sickness has no option but to be swallowed up in victory."*

21. Healing in Acts

A. Acts 1:1 AMP - "The first account I made, Theophilus, was [a continuous report] about all the things that Jesus began to do and to teach,"

B. Acts 3:6-8 AMP - "But Peter said, "Silver and gold I do not have; but what I do have I give to you: In the name (authority, power) of Jesus Christ the Nazarene—[begin now to] walk *and* go on walking!" Then he seized the man's right hand with a firm grip and raised him up. And at once his feet and ankles became strong *and* steady, and with a leap he stood up and *began* to walk; and he went into the temple with them, walking and leaping and praising God."

C. Acts 5:12 NKJV - "And through the hands of the apostles many signs and wonders were done among the people. And they were all with one accord in Solomon's Porch."

D. Acts 9:34 NKJV - "And Peter said to him, "Aeneas, Jesus the Christ heals you. Arise and make your bed." Then he arose immediately."

E. Acts 9:40 AMPC - "But Peter put them all out [of the room] and knelt down and prayed; then turning to the body he said, Tabitha, get up! And she opened her eyes; and when she saw Peter, she raised herself *and* sat upright."

F. Acts 19:11-12 AMP - "And God did unusual *and* extraordinary miracles by the hands of Paul, So that handkerchiefs *or* towels or aprons which had touched his skin were carried away *and* put upon the sick, and their diseases left them and the evil spirits came out of them."

Confession: *"Healing was not limited to Jesus' incarnation only but the scriptures testify that those who believe on the Lord will do the same works that He did and greater works. The ministry of the Holy Spirit and power as testified to in the book of Acts is available and active in my life today. The grace of God works with me granting that great signs and wonders be done in testimony to the preaching of the Gospel. Thank you Jesus that you have made your healing ministry available to me and in me today through the power of the Holy Spirit."*

22. Signs and Wonders

A. Mark 16:20 AMP - "And they went out and preached everywhere, while the Lord kept working with them and confirming the message by the attesting signs *and* miracles that closely accompanied [it]. Amen (so be it)."

B. Acts 3:6-8 AMP - "But Peter said, "Silver and gold I do not have; but what I do have I give to you: In the name (authority, power) of Jesus Christ the Nazarene—[begin now to] walk *and* go on walking!" Then he seized the man's right hand with a firm grip and raised him up. And at once his feet and ankles became strong *and* steady, and with a leap he stood up and *began* to walk; and he went into the temple with them, walking and leaping and praising God."

C. Acts 6:8 AMPC - "Now Stephen, full of grace (divine blessing and favor) and power (strength and ability) worked great wonders and signs (miracles) among the people."

D. Acts 14:3 NKJV - "Therefore they stayed there a long time, speaking boldly in the Lord, who was bearing witness to the word of His grace, granting signs and wonders to be done by their hands."

E. Hebrews 11:1 NKJV - "Now faith is the substance of things hoped for, the evidence of things not seen."

F. 1 Corinthians 12:9-11 NKJV - "to another faith by the same Spirit, to another gifts of healings by the same Spirit, to another the working of miracles, to another prophecy, to another discerning of spirits, to another *different* kinds of tongues, to another the interpretation of tongues. But one and the same Spirit works all these things, distributing to each one individually as He wills."

G. Romans 15:19 AMP - "[Even as my preaching has been accompanied] with the power of signs and wonders, [and all of it] by the power of the Holy Spirit. [The result is] that starting from Jerusalem and as far round as Illyricum, I have fully preached the Gospel [faithfully executing, accomplishing, carrying out to the full the good news] of Christ (the Messiah) in its entirety."

H. 2 Corinthians 12:12 AMP - "The signs that indicate a genuine apostle were performed among you fully *and* most patiently—signs and wonders and miracles."

I. 2 Corinthians 12:12 NKJV - "Truly the signs of an apostle were accomplished among you with all perseverance, in signs and wonders and mighty deeds."

Confession: *"Signs and Wonders work by the grace of God in my life. Thank you Heavenly Father, that you are glorified by granting that signs and wonders be done in the name of Jesus through believers like me. I embrace the grace of God to do what I cannot do in divine testimony to the truth of the Gospel. As I preach and testify to the Gospel I trust that the Holy Spirit is working miracles in all the hearers present. You will not let your children be put to shame."*

23. We are the Body of Christ

A. 1 Corinthians 12:12 AMP - "For just as the body is one and yet has many parts, and all the parts, though many, form [only] one body, so it is with Christ.

B. 1 Corinthians 6:15 AMP - "Do you not know that your bodies are members of Christ? Am I therefore to take the members of Christ and make them part of a prostitute? Certainly not!"
   I. My body was not made for sin, but for the Lord. My body was not made for sickness but for the Lord.
   II. My body is a member of Christ. Satan cannot make Christ's body sick.
   III. My body is the temple of Jehovah-Rapha, the Lord who heals me. He is healing me now.
   IV. Jesus' blood cleansed me from all sin, and by his stripes my body is healed.
   V. I glorify God in my body by refusing to allow disease any room in Jesus' name.

C. Ephesians 4:16 NKJV - "from whom the whole body, joined and knit together by what every joint supplies, according to the effective working by which every part does its share, causes growth of the body for the edifying of itself in love."

D. Matthew 21:12-14 NKJV - "Then Jesus went into the temple of God and drove out all those who bought and sold in the temple, and overturned the tables of the money changers and the seats of those who sold doves. And He said to them, "It is written, 'My house shall be called a house of prayer,' but you have made it a 'den of thieves.'" Then *the* blind and *the* lame came to Him in the temple, and He healed them.

E. 1 Thessalonians 5:23 AMP - "Now may the God of peace Himself sanctify you through and through [that is, separate you from profane and vulgar things, make you pure and whole and undamaged—consecrated to Him—set apart for His purpose]; and may your spirit and soul and body be kept complete and [be found] blameless at the coming of our Lord Jesus Christ."

Confession: *"I am a part of the body of Christ. The Holy Spirit is Lord over my body. Sickness, disease, and affliction have no more power over me as I have been crucified with Christ and am likewise raised to newness of life with Him. As the body of Christ I refuse every influence from the world or satan that would seek to corrupt what God has made to be incorrupt. My body is the temple of the Holy Spirit and I am securely joined together with other believers in the Body of which Christ is Head. Christ alone has power and authority over me. I submit to Christ's healing right now."*

24. We are the Temple of the Holy Spirit - Jesus the healer lives in me

A. 1 Corinthians 3:16-17 AMP - "Do you not know *and* understand that you [the church] are the temple of God, and that the Spirit of God dwells [permanently] in you [collectively and individually]? If anyone destroys the temple of God [corrupting it with false doctrine], God will destroy the destroyer; for the temple of God is holy (sacred), and that is what you are."

B. 2 Corinthians 4:7 NKJV - "But we have this treasure in earthen vessels, that the excellence of the power may be of God and not of us."

C. 1 John 4:4 AMP - "Little children (believers, dear ones), you are of God *and* you belong to Him and have [already] overcome them [the agents of the antichrist]; because He who is in you is greater than he (Satan) who is in the world [of sinful mankind]."

D. I am the Holy of Holies .

Confession: *"My body is the Temple of the Holy Spirit. Christ the Healer lives and operates in me. Greater is Christ in me than any opposing force in the world. The Temple of God is holy and sacred and in Christ that is what I am. My body is under the power of God and I submit now to His Lordship and care."*

25. My Body is to be Presented as a Living Sacrifice - I Separate myself to you Lord

A. Romans 12:1 AMP - "Therefore I urge you, brothers and sisters, by the mercies of God, to present your bodies [dedicating all of yourselves, set apart] as a living sacrifice, holy and well-pleasing to God, *which is* your rational (logical, intelligent) act of worship.

B. Malachi 1:8 AMP - "When you [priests] present the blind [animals] for sacrifice, is it not evil? And when you present the lame and the sick, is it not evil? Offer such a thing [as a blind or lame or sick animal] to your governor [as a gift or as payment for your taxes]. Would he be pleased with you? Or would he receive you graciously?" says the Lord of hosts."

C. Malachi 1:14 AMP - "But cursed is the swindler who has a male in his flock and vows [to offer] it, but sacrifices to the Lord a blemished *or* diseased thing! For I am a great King," says the Lord of hosts, "and My name is to be [reverently and greatly] feared among the nations."

D. Leviticus 22:17-20 AMP - "Then the Lord spoke to Moses, saying, "Speak to Aaron and his sons and to all the Israelites and say to them, 'Any man of the house of Israel or any stranger in Israel who presents his offering, whether to *fulfill* any of their vows or as any of their freewill (voluntary) offerings which they presented to the Lord as a burnt offering— so that you may be accepted—it must be a male without blemish from the cattle, the sheep, or the goats. You shall not offer anything which has a blemish, because it will not be accepted for you."

Confession: *"By the mercy of God I present my body as a living sacrifice. I walk in health and without blemish by the mercy of God and as an act of spiritual worship. I worship God in my body by receiving and walking in divine health and enablement. My gift to the Lord is not a dead and dying sacrifice but the alive and living sacrifice of my own life, for it is Christ who now lives in me and the life I live in this body is by faith in the Son of God who loves me."*

26. We are God's Priests

A. Revelation 1:6 NKJV - "and has made us kings and priests to His God and Father, to Him *be* glory and dominion forever and ever. Amen."

B. Revelation 5:10 AMP - "You have made them to be a kingdom [of royal subjects] and priests to our God; and they will reign on the earth."

C. Leviticus 21:4 NKJV - "*Otherwise* he shall not defile himself, *being* a chief man among his people, to profane himself."
   I. No defects!

D. Leviticus 21:18-21 NKJV - "For any man who has a defect shall not approach: a man blind or lame, who has a marred *face* or any *limb* too long, a man who has a broken foot or broken hand, or is a hunchback or a *dwarf*, or *a man* who has a defect in his eye, or eczema or scab, or is a eunuch. No man of the descendants of Aaron the priest, who has a defect, shall come near to offer the offerings made by fire to the Lord. He has a defect; he shall not come near to offer the bread of his God.

Confession: *"Whereas God has made me to be a priest to God He also has granted by his grace the enablement to fulfill the requirements of a priest. No man with a defect can serve as a priest. By the grace of God I receive healing and divine enablement to walk in the call of God upon my life to serve as a priest of God without defect."*

27. We are the Bride of Christ

A. Ephesians 5:26-27 AMP - "so that He might sanctify the church, having cleansed her by the washing of water with the word [of God], so that [in turn] He might present the church to Himself in glorious splendor, without spot or wrinkle or any such thing; but that she would be holy [set apart for God] and blameless."

B. Hebrews 10:22 AMP - "let us approach [God] with a true *and* sincere heart in unqualified assurance of faith, having had our hearts sprinkled *clean* from an evil conscience and our bodies washed with pure water."

C. Song of Solomon 4:7 NKJV - "You *are* all fair, my love, And *there is* no spot in you."

D. Song of Solomon 5:9 NKJV - "What *is* your beloved More than *another* beloved, O fairest among women? What *is* your beloved More than *another* beloved, That you so charge us?"

Confession: *"God will present the church to Himself in glorious splendor, without spot or wrinkle or any defect. As a member of the church of God I receive the ministry of the washing of water with the word of God to sanctify and cleanse me of all defects and weakness. God's love for me brings complete healing."*

28. He is the Vine, We are the Branches

A. John 15:1-8 AMP - "I am the true Vine, and My Father is the vinedresser. Every branch in Me that does not bear fruit, He takes away; and every *branch* that continues to bear fruit, He [repeatedly] prunes, so that it will bear more fruit [even richer and finer fruit]. You are already clean because of the word which I have given you [the teachings which I have discussed with you]. Remain in Me, and I [will remain] in you. Just as no branch can bear fruit by itself without remaining in the vine, neither can you [bear fruit, producing evidence of your faith] unless you remain in Me. I am the Vine; you are the branches. The one who remains in Me and I in him bears much fruit, for [otherwise] apart from Me [that is, cut off from vital union with Me] you can do nothing. If anyone does not remain in Me, he is thrown out like a [broken off] branch, and withers *and* dies; and they gather such branches and throw them into the fire, and they are burned. If you remain in Me and My words remain in you [that is, if we are vitally united and My message lives in your heart], ask whatever you wish and it will be done for you. My Father is glorified *and* honored by this, when you bear much fruit, and prove yourselves to be My [true] disciples."

B. Luke 6:43-44 NKJV - "For a good tree does not bear bad fruit, nor does a bad tree bear good fruit. For every tree is known by its own fruit. For *men* do not gather figs from thorns, nor do they gather grapes from a bramble bush."

C. Revelation 22:2 AMP - "in the middle of its street. On either side of the river was the tree of life, bearing twelve *kinds of* fruit, yielding its fruit every month; and the leaves of the tree were for the healing of the nations."

Confession: *"I am a branch of the true vine. I am connected to God in Christ and receive my life and nourishment from God. My life and fruitfulness depend on the Lord. As I am planted in the Lord and my life comes from Him, I likewise receive healing and deliverance from him for all that afflicts or oppresses me. I am connected to God and my body reaps the benefits of the true vine."*

29. God Promises us Long Life - Zoe (Abundant Life)

A. Psalms 91:10-16 NKJV - "No evil shall befall you, Nor shall any plague come near your dwelling; For He shall give His angels charge over you, To keep you in all your ways. In *their* hands they shall bear you up, Lest you dash your foot against a stone. You shall tread upon the lion and the cobra, The young lion and the serpent you shall trample underfoot. "Because he has set his love upon Me, therefore I will deliver him; I will set him on high, because he has known My name. He shall call upon Me, and I will answer him; I *will be* with him in trouble; I will deliver him and honor him. With long life I will satisfy him, And show him My salvation."

B. Proverbs 11:28 AMP - "He who leans on *and* trusts in *and* is confident in his riches will fall, But the righteous [who trust in God's provision] will flourish like a *green* leaf."

C. Proverbs 3:1-2 NKJV - "My son, do not forget my law, But let your heart keep my commands; For length of days and long life And peace they will add to you."

D. Proverbs 3:16 AMP - "Long life is in her right hand; In her left hand are riches and honor."

E. Proverbs 14:1 NKJV - "The wise woman builds her house, But the foolish pulls it down with her hands."

F. Proverbs 10:27 AMP - "The [reverent] fear of the Lord [worshiping, obeying, serving, and trusting Him with awe-filled respect] prolongs one's life, But the years of the wicked will be shortened."

G. Proverbs 12:28 AMPC - "Life is in the way of righteousness (moral and spiritual rectitude in every area and relation), and in its pathway there is no death *but* immortality (perpetual, eternal life)."

H. Proverbs 9:11 NKJV - "For by me your days will be multiplied, And years of life will be added to you."

I. Romans 8:2 NKJV - "For the law of the Spirit of life in Christ Jesus has made me free from the law of sin and death."

J. Romans 8:11 NKJV - "But if the Spirit of Him who raised Jesus from the dead dwells in you, He who raised Christ from the dead will also give life to your mortal bodies through His Spirit who dwells in you."

    I. The Spirit of God is residing in me. He has made his home in my spirit.

    II. The Spirit of the Lord who heals me is creating and supplying life in my body now.

    III. The life of Jehovah-Rapha is being applied to my body by his spirit who dwells in me.

    IV. The life of God drives out every trace of sickness and disease, destroying every parasite and germ that would harm my body.

K. Habakuk 1:12 AMP - "Are You not from everlasting, O Lord, my God, My Holy One? We will not die. O Lord, You have appointed the Chaldeans [who rule in Babylon] to execute [Your] judgment, And You, O Rock, have established them to correct *and* chastise."

Confession: *"My life is hidden with Christ in God. All the days of my life are in God's hands. The Lord gives life to those who rely, trust, and depend on him. The Law of the Spirit of Life in Christ Jesus has set me free from the Law of Sin and the Law of Death. No man takes my life, but I have laid it down with Christ and God has raised it up again. I trust in the Lord to prolong and extend my days for as long as He pleases."*

30. God's Exclusive Promises

A. 2 Corinthians 2:14 NKJV - "Now thanks *be* to God who always leads us in triumph in Christ, and through us diffuses the fragrance of His knowledge in every place."

B. Colossians 1:12-14 NKJV - "giving thanks to the Father who has qualified us to be partakers of the inheritance of the saints in the light. He has delivered us from the power of darkness and conveyed *us* into the kingdom of the Son of His love, in whom we have redemption through His blood, the forgiveness of sins."
   I. I am qualified, entitled, worthy, and able to partake of my inheritance in Christ.
   II. Healing belongs to me (Psalms 103:3), I refuse to be beaten out of my inheritance.
   III. I have been delivered from the authority of darkness. I have been delivered from Satan's authority and dominion (Acts 26:18). Therefore Satan can't dominate me with sickness and disease.
   IV. I have passed out of Satan's jurisdiction and over into the Kingdom of the Son of God. I am a citizen in the Kingdom of Jehovah-Rapha, the Lord who heals me.

V. In Christ Jesus I have redemption. I am delivered from satan and his works of sickness and disease.

C. Psalms 34:9 AMP - "O [reverently] fear the Lord, you His saints (believers, holy ones); For to those who fear Him there is no want."

D. Psalms 34:17 NKJV - "*The righteous* cry out, and the Lord hears, And delivers them out of all their troubles."

E. Psalms 34:19 AMP - "Many hardships *and* perplexing circumstances confront the righteous, But the Lord rescues him from them all."

F. Matthew 18:18 AMP - " I assure you *and* most solemnly say to you, whatever you bind [forbid, declare to be improper and unlawful] on earth shall have [already] been bound in heaven, and whatever you loose [permit, declare lawful] on earth shall have [already] been loosed in heaven."

G. John 14:13-14 NKJV - "And whatever you ask in My name, that I will do, that the Father may be glorified in the Son. If you ask anything in My name, I will do *it.*"

H. Hebrews 11:39-40 AMP - "And all of these, though they gained [divine] approval through their faith, did not receive [the fulfillment of] what was promised, because God had us in mind *and* had something better for us, so that they [these men and women of authentic faith] would not be made perfect [that is, completed in Him] apart from us."

Confession: *"I have passed out of Satan's jurisdiction and over into the Kingdom of the Son of God. I am a citizen in the Kingdom of the Lord who heals. Whatever I ask in Jesus' authority is done by Jesus for the glory of the Father."*

31. God's Glory Within

A. Colossians 1:27 AMP - "God [in His eternal plan] chose to make known to them how great for the Gentiles are the riches of the glory of this mystery, which is Christ in *and* among you, the hope *and* guarantee of [realizing the] glory.

B. 2 Corinthians 3:18 NKJV - "But we all, with unveiled face, beholding as in a mirror the glory of the Lord, are being transformed into the same image from glory to glory, just as by the Spirit of the Lord.
  I. "I am the Light of Glory."

C. Malachi 4:1-3 AMP - "For behold, the day is coming, burning like a furnace, and all the arrogant (proud, self-righteous, haughty), and every evildoer shall be stubble; and the day that is coming shall set them on fire," says the Lord of hosts, "so that it will leave them neither root nor branch. But for you who fear My name [with awe-filled reverence] the sun of righteousness will rise with healing in its wings. And you will go forward and leap [joyfully] like calves [released] from the stall. You will trample the wicked, for they will be ashes under the soles of your feet on the day that I do this," says the Lord of hosts."

      I. The Sun of Righteousness has arisen, having conquered sickness and satan. There is healing in his wings.

     II. That healing is beaming into me now by his word. I am trusting beneath his healing wings.

D. John 17:22-24 NKJV - "And the glory which You gave Me I have given them, that they may be one just as We are one: I in them, and You in Me; that they may be made perfect in one, and that the world may know that You have sent Me, and have loved them as You have loved Me. "Father, I desire that they also whom You gave Me may be with Me where I am, that they may behold My glory which You have given Me; for You loved Me before the foundation of the world."

E. Romans 2:7 NKJV - "eternal life to those who by patient continuance in doing good seek for glory, honor, and immortality;"

F. 2 Timothy 1:10 AMP - "but now [that extraordinary purpose and grace] has been fully disclosed *and* realized by us through the appearing of our Savior Christ Jesus who [through His incarnation and earthly ministry] abolished death [making it null and void] and brought life and immortality to light through the gospel,"

Confession: *"I am being transformed by the Spirit of the Lord from glory to glory. The glory of God in me bears witness to the fact that Christ Jesus abolished death and brought life and immortality to light through the gospel."*

32. Appointment in the Church

A. 1 Corinthians 12:28 NKJV - "And God has appointed these in the church: first apostles, second prophets, third teachers, after that miracles, then gifts of healings, helps, administrations, varieties of tongues."

Confession: *"God has appointed gifts of healings in the church. Healing and miracles are God's will and God's gift to the church. Healing is the children's bread."*

33. Christ is Healing

A. John 5:24 AMP - "I assure you *and* most solemnly say to you, the person who hears My word [the one who heeds My message], and believes *and* trusts in Him who sent Me, has (possesses now) eternal life [that is, eternal life actually begins—the believer is transformed], and does not come into judgment *and* condemnation, but has passed [over] from death into life."

B. John 6:33 NKJV - "For the bread of God is He who comes down from heaven and gives life to the world."

C. John 6:58 AMP - "This is the Bread which came down out of heaven. It is not like [the manna that] our fathers ate and they [eventually] died; the one who eats this Bread [believes in Me, accepts Me as Savior] will live forever."

D. 1 Corinthians 1:30 NKJV - "But of Him you are in Christ Jesus, who became for us wisdom from God—and righteousness and sanctification and redemption— "

E. Malachi 4:2 AMP - "But for you who fear My name [with awe-filled reverence] the sun of righteousness will rise with healing in its wings. And you will go forward and leap [joyfully] like calves [released] from the stall."

Confession: *"Christ is my light and my salvation. In Christ I have passed over from death into life. Christ is my savior from death who causes me to live forever."*

34. Divine Protection

A. Psalms 91: 1-6 AMP - "He who dwells in the shelter of the Most High Will remain secure *and* rest in the shadow of the Almighty [whose power no enemy can withstand]. I will say of the Lord, "He is my refuge and my fortress, My God, in whom I trust [with great confidence, and on whom I rely]!" For He will save you from the trap of the fowler, And from the deadly pestilence. He will cover you *and* completely protect you with His pinions, And under His wings you will find refuge; His faithfulness is a shield and a wall. You will not be afraid of the terror of night, Nor of the arrow that flies by day, Nor of the pestilence that stalks in darkness, Nor of the destruction (sudden death) that lays waste at noon.

B. Psalms 91:10 NKJV - "No evil shall befall you, Nor shall any plague come near your dwelling;"
  I. I am abiding under the shadow (oversight) of the Almighty.
  II. Jehovah-Rapha, the Lord who heals me, is my refuge and fortress against disease.
  III. His word is my shield and buckler against sickness.
  IV. I'm trusting under his wings. There is healing in his wings (Malachi 4:1)

- V. I'm not afraid of disease. I'm not afraid of sickness.
- VI. No plague shall come near my dwelling or my body.
- VII. Say: "Sickness, you shall not come near my body. I refuse you."

C. James 4:7 NKJV - "Therefore submit to God. Resist the devil and he will flee from you."
   - I. I submit to the will of God. I accept the authority of God and his word.
   - II. Say: "I submit to God's word. I resist you, Devil. I resist disease. Get out! You must flee my body now."

D. Proverbs 11:8 AMP - "The righteous is rescued from trouble, And the wicked takes his place."

E. Psalms 34:19 AMP - "Many hardships *and* perplexing circumstances confront the righteous, But the Lord rescues him from them all."

Confession: *"My life and health are subject to the divine protection and promises of God. The Lord rescues me continually from all hardships and trials. The Lord is my refuge from sickness and disease. No plague comes near me."*

35. In Giving

A. Malachi 3:10-12 AMP - "Bring all the tithes (the tenth) into the storehouse, so that there may be food in My house, and test Me now in this," says the Lord of hosts, "if I will not open for you the windows of heaven and pour out for you [so great] a blessing until there is no more room to receive it. Then I will rebuke the devourer (insects, plague) for your sake and he will not destroy the fruits of the ground, nor will your vine in the field drop *its grapes* [before harvest]," says the Lord of hosts. "All nations shall call you happy *and* blessed, for you shall be a land of delight," says the Lord of hosts."

B. Recommended teaching from SMI: "Can you buy a Miracle?"

C. Giving is operating in the nature of God
   I. John 3:16 "For God so loved…that he gave."
   II. When we give we participate in God's grace by imitating God who is a giver.

D. 2 Kings chapter 4 relates the story of a wealthy woman who made provision for the man of God. This came back to her in miracles.

E. 2 Corinthians 9:6-8 NKJV - "But this *I say:* He who sows sparingly will also reap sparingly, and he who sows bountifully will also reap bountifully. *So let* each one *give* as he purposes in his heart, not grudgingly or of necessity; for God loves a cheerful giver. And God *is* able to make all grace abound toward you, that you, always having all sufficiency in all *things,* may have an abundance for every good work."
  I. God makes all grace abound toward you.
  II. Divine influence for your healing abounds.

Confession: *"I have put off the old nature with it's selfishness and lust and have put on the new nature with it's generosity and charity. I am an imitator of Christ and God's grace is working with me every day. Neither satan nor the world have any say in my health. I will not let any part of my being participate in the work of the old, selfish nature and frustrate grace in my life. I give to others because God has given to me. God is a giver and I am a giver."*

About the Author

Warren Hunter is the Founder and President of Sword Ministries International. Born in South Africa, he was raised under the influence of many well known ministers. At the age of thirteen, he began a ministry leading weekly Bible studies for his fellow students. After arriving in America, he received seven years of higher education in Tulsa, Oklahoma, which included Oral Roberts University.

In 1988 Sword Ministries International was launched as a Non-Profit Organization. Through ministering on the streets, traveling weekends, writing books, and much prayer, Warren's ministry has expanded within the call of God on his life.

To date Warren has authored more than twenty five books and teaching manuals and has dozens of teaching series as well as hundreds of individual audio teachings. As a young boy in South Africa, he assisted his grandfather Bernard Hunter in building many churches. Warren has seen thousands come to Christ not only in South Africa, but worldwide through this ministry and especially in Central Africa over the last decade.

Today, He lives in Branson, Missouri with his wife and six children. Warren is an internationally known speaker who conducts hundreds of meetings every year in addition to a daily live streamed bible study. His vision is to touch the world with a vibrant and unlimited move of God, effecting lasting changes in hearts and lives with signs and wonders following decently and in order by the power of the Holy Spirit.

Apostolic Sword Network

As you read through the ASN Manual, you will begin to see Apostolic Revivalist Warren Hunter's heart for kingdom connections and pure covenant father-son relationships.

As a member of ASN you are a member of the Sword Ministries International family and are a part of the big picture as we touch the world through a vibrant move of the power and demonstration of God's Spirit through signs, wonders and miracles.

Within the manual you will also find information about being licensed and/or ordained through the Apostolic Sword Network. Please visit the Five Pillar Visionary Structure to see the *bigness* of the vision that God has for Sword Ministries International and how you can be a part of it!

Once you have read and prayed through the manual, you may contact us and we will answer any other questions you may have.

Find the *Apostolic Sword Network Manual* for free online at: www.swordministries.org/apostolic-sword-network

Sword Ministries Resource Library

Books

- 35 Reasons Healing is God's Will
- Divine Attraction
- From Fire to Glory
- God Working With God
- Growing in Confidence
- How to Birth a Miracle
- Is Your Perception a Weapon
- Keys to a Yielded Will
- Presenting a Yielded Will
- Supply of the Spirit
- The Breath of the Almighty
- The Glory of the Anointing
- The Lightenings of God
- The Power of a Consecrated Heart
- The Power of Innocence
- The Vision of the Seed
- The Weightiness of God
- Think Like God
- Touch Not my Anointed
- Transparency
- Unlimited Realm Vol. 1
- Unlimited Realm Vol. 2
- Visionaries: Rise to Leadership
- Visionaries: Set Your Sights Higher
- Walking on Water

Audio Series

- Awakening Prophetic Purpose
- Divine Attraction
- Faith 101
- Faith for Life
- First Fruits
- Force of a Recreated Spirit
- God Hears Himself
- God Working With God Vol 1
- Grace for Life
- Holy Spirit in the Old Covenant
- I Am Who I Am
- Jesus Like Leadership
- Kingdom Power
- Living in the Cloud
- Love Defined
- Nature of Miracles
- New Wine
- Raising Warriors in a Cave
- The Fragrance of Christ
- The Secret of God
- Tuning in to the Voice of God
- Uncapping the Forces of God Within
- Who are You? ID in Christ

Training Manuals + DVD

- Called to Call
- Concerning Spirituals
- Flowing in the Supernatural
- Focus
- Increase the Anointing
- Leading with Power through Apostolic Thrust
- The Prophetic Spirit
- Supernatural Leadership Training Institute
- Wisdom for Signs and Wonders

These and much more available through the Sword Ministries web store: **www.swordministries.org**

Sword Ministries International

For information or further resources please contact Sword Ministries through the following channels.

Write to:

Sword Ministries International
P.O. Box 7360
Branson, MO 65616

Email:
info@swordministries.org

Website:
www.swordministries.org

US Ministry Office:
(417) 544 - 0838

Social Media:
Find us on **Facebook**, **Youtube**, **LinkedIn**, etc

www.ingramcontent.com/pod-product-compliance
Lightning Source LLC
Chambersburg PA
CBHW071259040426
42444CB00009B/1786